My Life with Tourette Syndrome

written by **Mari Schuh** • art by **Ana Sebastián**

AMICUS ILLUSTRATED is published by Amicus
P.O. Box 227, Mankato, MN 56002
www.amicuspublishing.us

Editor: Rebecca Glaser
Series Designer: Kathleen Petelinsek
Book Designer: Lori Bye

Library of Congress Cataloging-in-Publication Data
Names: Schuh, Mari C., 1975- author. | Sebastián, Ana, illustrator.
Title: My life with tourette syndrome / by Mari Schuh ; illustrated by Ana Sebastián.
Description: Mankato, Minnesota : Amicus Learning, [2024] | Series: My life with... | Includes bibliographical references. |
Audience: Ages 6–9 | Audience: Grades 2–3 | Summary: "Meet Emma! She loves riding roller coasters and playing at the
beach. She also has Tourette syndrome. Emma is real and so are her experiences. Learn about her life in this
illustrated narrative nonfiction picture book for elementary students"—Provided by publisher.
Identifiers: LCCN 2022045658 (print) | LCCN 2022045659 (ebook) |
ISBN 9781645494898 (library binding) | ISBN 9781681528960 (paperback) | ISBN 9781645494935 (ebook)
Subjects: LCSH: Tourette syndrome in children—Juvenile literature. |
Tourette syndrome in children—Patients—United States—Biography—Juvenile literature.
Classification: LCC RJ496.T68 S38 2024 (print) | LCC RJ496.T68 (ebook) |
DDC 618.92/83--dc23/eng/20221007
LC record available at https://lccn.loc.gov/2022045658
LC ebook record available at https://lccn.loc.gov/2022045659

For Emma and her family—MS

About the Author
Mari Schuh's love of reading began with cereal boxes at
the kitchen table. Today she is the author of hundreds of
nonfiction books for beginning readers. With each book, Mari
hopes she's helping kids learn a little bit more about the world
around them. Find out more about her at marischuh.com.

About the Illustrator
Ana Sebastián is an illustrator living in Spain. She studied
Fine Arts at University of Zaragoza and Université Michel de
Montaigne, Bordeaux. Specializing in digital illustration, she
completed her education with a master's degree in digital
illustration for concept art and visual development.

Hello! My name is Emma. I'm a smart, fun kid. We might like the same things. I like to ride roller coasters and play at the beach. We might have differences, too. I have Tourette syndrome. Let me tell you about my life.

Tourette syndrome causes people to have tics. Tics are sudden, short movements or sounds. Tics happen again and again. Doctors do not know what causes Tourette syndrome.

People have different tics. Some people grunt. Others blink their eyes. They might quickly move their body. I jump and skip. I smack my lips. Some people say swear words. But that is not common. Tics are kind of like sneezes, hiccups, or coughs. People might try to stop them. But they cannot be controlled.

When I was seven years old, I cleared my throat again and again. My mom and dad asked me to stop. But I couldn't stop. I repeated words and giggled. I also tightened my stomach muscles.

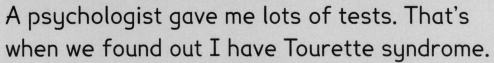

A psychologist gave me lots of tests. That's when we found out I have Tourette syndrome.

Tics can be hard to notice. My family learned that I had been having tics since I was very young. I smelled my hands. I jumped and skipped. I also made faces.

People with Tourette syndrome often have other disorders, too. I have ADHD. That's attention deficit hyperactivity disorder. I also have OCD, which is obsessive-compulsive disorder. I have anxiety, too. I talk with a therapist. She helps me.

My disorders make me have a lot of energy.
My body always wants to move.

Being active helps me relax.
Then I have fewer tics.

Sometimes I try to stop my tics. But that can make them worse. It is better to let tics happen. I worry about what people think about me. But I don't let my tics stop me from doing things I like. I'm good at soccer.

Many things can make a person have tics more often. These are called triggers. Mine include being tired or upset or when plans suddenly change. Today, soccer practice was canceled. That made me have tics.

When I started a new school, I cleared my throat a lot. My classmates heard me. They asked me to stop. I said, sorry, I can't stop. A few of them did not believe me.

My mom and dad made a booklet for my classmates. It helped them understand me. The next day, a classmate gave me a gift. It was a seashell. Others said they were sorry.

My teachers are kind to me. They know that I need breaks. They let me go for short walks. Then I come back to my classroom. My favorite class is art. I love to draw.

I don't want to get rid of my Tourette syndrome. I love myself just the way I am. My family does, too. Tourette syndrome makes me special. After all, everyone is different in some way. If we were all the same, the world would not be as fun!

20

Meet Emma

Hi! I'm Emma. I am friendly, kind, and loving. I live in California with my mom, dad, and sister. I like to make art and play video games. Skateboarding and playing soccer are fun, too. I am a goalie on my soccer team. I am also a Girl Scout and a junior youth ambassador for the Tourette Association of America.

Respecting People with Tourette Syndrome

When someone with Tourette syndrome is having a tic, be patient. Some tics last several seconds. Others last a few minutes.

Remember that people cannot stop a tic. Do not ask them to stop.

Be respectful of people with Tourette syndrome. Do not make fun of them or stare at them.

Treat people with Tourette syndrome like you would any other person. Accept them and like them for who they are.

Sometimes tics can be hard to notice. When someone tells you they have Tourette syndrome, believe them.

Kids with Tourette syndrome want to have fun, just like all kids do. Be sure to invite them to play with you.

Helpful Terms

ADHD A disorder that makes it hard for people to pay attention, sit still, and listen. ADHD stands for attention deficit hyperactivity disorder.

anxiety A feeling of worry or fear.

OCD An anxiety disorder that causes people to have stressful thoughts, habits, and fears. OCD stands for obsessive-compulsive disorder.

psychologist A person who studies people's minds, emotions, and behavior.

therapist A person who is trained to help people with conditions, disorders, and illnesses learn new skills.

tic A sudden, repeated movement or sound that cannot be controlled.

trigger Something that might cause someone have tics more often.

Read More

Mederos, Melissa. **Tic & Twitch: A Story About Tourette Syndrome.**
Miami: Millennial Publishing Co., 2022.

Pettiford, Rebecca. **Showing Kindness.** Minneapolis: Jump!, 2018.

Schuh, Mari. **My Life with ADHD.** Mankato, Minn.: Amicus, 2021.

Websites

CDC: KIDS' QUEST: TOURETTE SYNDROME

https://www.cdc.gov/ncbddd/kids/tourette.html

Quiz yourself to see what you know about Tourette syndrome and then learn more about it.

KIDSHEALTH: TOURETTE SYNDROME

https://kidshealth.org/en/kids/k-tourette.html

An easy-to-read overview of Tourette syndrome.

TOURETTE ASSOCIATION OF AMERICA: STORIES THAT INSPIRE

https://tourette.org/about-tourette/stories-that-inspire/

Read personal stories about people who have Tourette syndrome.

Every effort has been made to ensure that these websites are appropriate for children. However, because of the nature of the Internet, it is impossible to guarantee that these sites will remain active indefinitely or that their contents will not be altered.